Original title:
Sands of Serenity

Copyright © 2025 Creative Arts Management OÜ
All rights reserved.

Author: Eleanor Prescott
ISBN HARDBACK: 978-1-80581-590-7
ISBN PAPERBACK: 978-1-80581-117-6
ISBN EBOOK: 978-1-80581-590-7

Footprints of Peace

In the beach's soft embrace, a dance of feet,
I lost my flip-flops, now I'm feeling beat.
Seagulls laugh while I hop on one leg,
Chasing a crab, it's quite the hilarious peg.

Sunshine tickles my nose, I grin like a fool,
Surfboards wobble, who made those rules?
Children giggle, building castles so grand,
While I trip over my own sunburnt hand.

Serenity in Grain

A grain of sand with a story to tell,
It whispered to me, 'Boy, this is swell!'
I squished it between my toes just for fun,
It said, 'You should try this—oh, isn't it pun?'

Kites in the air, tangled like my hair,
The wind has taken them, they're beyond repair.
I wave at my neighbors, they wave back too,
In the battle of laughter, we all claim our due.

Horizon's Gentle Caress

The horizon winks, it's a cheeky affair,
Brushes my worries with a sun-kissed flair.
I squint at the waves, they're giggling too,
Playing tag with shells, a real hullabaloo!

A seagull swoops down, squawks like it's mad,
"Hey there, buddy! Stop looking so sad!"
A dance with the breeze, it pulls me away,
Life's a big joke on this bright sunny day.

Solitude's Warm Embrace

Alone on this stretch, I sip from my cup,
The wind brings a laugh, as I lift it up.
My sandwich flies off, a gusty delight,
The gulls plan their heist, oh, what a sight!

I throw them a crumb; they scramble and fight,
A comedy show, under the warm sunlight.
With laughter I stroll, footprints left behind,
In this jocular joy, peace is what I find.

Whispers of the Dunes

A turtle wearing shades, oh so bright,
Sips ice-cold lemonade, what a sight!
He nods at the lizards, a snazzy crew,
Plotting the next dance, the funky two-step too.

The cacti wave hands, in their prickly way,
As tumbleweeds tumble, they join the ballet.
With a laugh and a jest, under the sun,
Even the scorpions know how to have fun!

Echoes in the Desert Wind

A breeze tells tales of a long-lost shoe,
It danced with the chips from a taco or two.
The sun wearing goggles is quite a sight,
While cacti compete in a sunbathing fight.

The owls hoot jokes, they're quite the wise guys,
As lizards in bow ties do quick little flies.
Under stars so bright, they share hearty laughs,
With sandstorm shenanigans and silly gaffs.

Tranquil Horizons

A hammock swings low in the warm desert air,
Where lizards lounge back without a care.
The owls hold a meeting on top of a rock,
Discussing hot gossip—can you believe this talk?

Walking a pet snake that thinks it's a cat,
Makes for a sight that's old hat gone flat.
While shadows grow long, and moonbeams glow bright,
Their telepathy's clear—each silly delight!

Mirage of Stillness

In a pond made of pixel, fish wear a wig,
Telling tall tales of the big, funny gig.
A cactus with shades gives a cool little wink,
While palm trees roll dice and start to rethink.

The sand dunes raise hands, in a wave of surprise,
As camels in tuxes dance under the skies.
Their two-step goes wild, it's truly the best,
In this endless expanse, they throw a wild fest!

Hushed Horizons Beneath the Vast

In a world where seagulls laugh out loud,
The waves roll in, a joyful crowd.
Flip-flops flying, kids in disarray,
The beach is where we tumble and play.

Sandcastle kingdoms, a grand charade,
Moat filled with water, a splash crusade.
But a sneaky wave, oh what a prank,
Turns our fortress into a soggy flank.

Sunburnt noses with shades askew,
We champion ketchup and mustard too.
Picnic blanket transformed to a trap,
With ants holding a dance-off on our lap!

Life's salty breezes fill up our sails,
On dodgy inflatable, we swap our tales.
With every splash and giggle around,
We find joy profound on this sandy ground.

A Canvas of Stillness Beneath the Cosmos

Under starlit skies, we lay so low,
Chasing fireflies with a clumsy glow.
Blankets tangled in our nighttime spree,
We giggle and squirm, a sight to see.

The snacks we brought, a riotous mix,
Popcorn exploded, oh what a fix!
Chocolate melting on every face,
We're a chaotic, sugary embrace.

In the corner, the crickets play tunes,
While we're arguing over the best cartoons.
With marshmallow battles and silly jokes,
This canvas glimmers with laughter strokes.

As the moon winks, casting funny shadows,
We take silly photos, making amigos.
In this quiet, giggly starlight ballet,
We're the stars of our own wild play.

Fleeting Moments of Pure Ease

A hammock sways like a browser's page,
Time's slipping by, we're all in a daze.
With sodas in hand and laughter galore,
We promise this moment, we want more!

Flip-flops and sunscreen, forget about fate,
We're here for the snacks piled high on our plate.
Each chip is a treasure, each dip is a dream,
In the sun's warm glow, we're a silly team.

The breeze carries whispers of half-baked plans,
Like starting a band with our kitchen pans.
We strum on cucumbers, drum on the floor,
Who knew salad could bring so much more?

As dusk settles in, our giggles float high,
With fireflies agreeing to help us comply.
No worries or work, just the sweet and the ease,
In these fleeting moments, we do what we please!

Sanctuary in the Golden Twilight

As daylight dips into a golden hug,
We gather around like a big cozy bug.
With each bonfire popping a playful spark,
We roast each other like hot dogs in the dark.

The sunset winks, casting shadows wide,
Silly songs bubble, we won't be denied.
Off-key harmonies explode in the air,
We don't mind the pitch, just the love we share.

With marshmallows ready for laughter's feast,
We'd trade the quiet for fun, not the least.
Sticky hands joined in the twilight's reign,
We're a family of joy, together in the plain.

So here's to the dusk and its playful charms,
Finding our haven in each other's arms.
As the stars awaken, our giggles ignite,
This sanctuary feels oh-so-right!

Pebbles of Peace Beneath Footsteps

In a world where shoes just squeak,
And toes wiggle, oh so meek.
Each pebble laughs beneath my feet,
As ticklish stones offer a treat.

A flip-flop's clash, a sandal dance,
Every step, a chance to prance.
Who knew that rocks could be so sly,
Whispering giggles as I pass by?

The tiny ones have witty charm,
They take no heed of sun or harm.
With every tumble, they conspire,
To tickle toes, ignite desire.

So I wander, joyfully lost,
In a playground where no one's bossed.
With shoes off, I find my delight,
Among the pebbles that shine so bright.

Moments Caught in Silver Dust

Dust bunnies dance like tiny dreams,
Spinning secrets, or so it seems.
Moments lost in twirls of light,
Who knew dust could hold such delight?

A sneeze erupts, the laughter flies,
While feathery flakes fall from the skies.
Caught in the webs of playful glances,
Beneath the beams, we make our trances.

Every shimmer tells a tale,
Of wayward socks and paper trails.
In corners where the shadows play,
Lies joy wrapped in yesterday's spray.

So let us twirl in this fine mess,
Embracing chaos, we'll never stress.
With every sparkle in the air,
Life turns silly without a care.

Serendipity among Shifting Mounds

Little hills, oh what a sight,
That wobble, wiggle, full of light.
I trip and tumble, what a show,
A stumble here, a roll, then whoa!

Each mound whispers, 'Come and play!'
So off I go, I can't delay.
With laughter ringing down the slope,
Every misstep fuels a new hope.

A friendly roll, a sudden slide,
Gravity working as my guide.
With every rise, a silly grin,
Here's joy residing deep within.

So if you find the ground gets steep,
Forget the worry, take a leap!
For in each mound, life's giggles stir,
Where serendipity will not defer.

The Quietude of Time's Embrace

Tick-tock whispers, oh so sly,
As moments pass and time slips by.
Sitting still, I hold my breath,
In the quiet, laughs come to rest.

The clock's soft chuckle warms the day,
With every tick, it seems to play.
Forgotten chores just drift away,
As time and I have a ballet.

A sip of tea, the giggles creep,
In solitude where secrets keep.
So let the hours sway and tease,
In quietude, I find my ease.

Among the minutes, subtle and fine,
I throw my cares to the vine.
In this stillness, laughter breeds,
And joy, like sunlight, gently feeds.

Caresses of Twilight on Soft Horizons

A cat sat on a hat, all gray,
With dreams of fish, so far away.
He swayed his tail, a gentle grace,
While evening played on his cheeky face.

The moon looked down, all round and bright,
As stars danced high, a comical sight.
A cow mooed softly, not quite in time,
While frogs croaked tunes like big bells chime.

A breeze tickled leaves, they laughed aloud,
Bringing giggles from the cloud.
The dusk wore a grin, so sly and sweet,
As shadows twirled to a soft beat.

So raise a glass to the night so bold,
With secrets Nonsense waiting to unfold.
For humor's found in the twilight glow,
As jests collide like waves below.

Spheres of Calma Amidst Restless Waves

A fish in a suit, all dressed for tea,
Pondered if bubbles were good for me.
It twirled through the tides, with grace and style,
While crabs played poker, alluding a smile.

The pelicans danced, with one on a call,
Who tripped on a net and began to fall.
They quacked with glee, a silly ballet,
As dolphins laughed in their own playful way.

A hammock was strung 'tween two seagull wings,
Where a lazy old dog tried out his things.
He snorted and snored as the waves swayed him,
Dreaming of treasures, his light heart and whim.

Laughter surged like a wave on the shore,
With each funny tale, we just begged for more.
So let's splash in the silliness we've made,
In waters where chuckles and joy parade.

Timeless Whispers in Endless Fields

Grasshoppers played hopscotch at dawn,
While daisies were scheming, with mischief drawn.
A goat wore glasses, reading the news,
And bumbled through poems with silly views.

The wind told tales, with a wink and a swirl,
Of tumbling kittens and dancing squirrels.
A kite flopped low, in a tumble so grand,
As frogs cheered it on, a quirk for the band.

Sunflowers chuckled as shadows unfold,
While twirling in breezes, so daring and bold.
The farmer, perplexed, checked his hat for bees,
As crickets recited their spry melodies.

With giggling blooms that sway and tease,
Nature's punchlines flow with the breeze.
In fields where laughter weaves through the air,
Every little moment becomes a grand affair.

The Peace Found in Nature's Embrace

A squirrel ached for a nap in the sun,
He tried counting nuts, but just found one.
As bees buzzed softly, a riddle to share,
His dreams took flight, floating everywhere.

The clouds blew kisses, all fluffy and white,
While a raccoon juggled, oh what a sight!
Worms plotted schemes, in the garden's embrace,
And played hide-and-seek, a comical race.

A turtle on skates scooted round and round,
Searching for treasures, that couldn't be found.
His friends roared in laughter, a sight so sublime,
As the tree branches joined him, just in time.

In nature's wide arms, we find quiet cheer,
Where humor's a balm, bringing smiles near.
So let the world giggle, in joy's warm space,
In the heart of life, where laughter takes place.

Threads of Calm in a Turbulent World

In a world that twirls with flair,
I balance on a giant chair.
The cat, he jumps, I lose my grip,
And down I go – a graceful trip!

While winds of chaos swirl around,
I wear my socks, both green and brown.
A dance of laundry, socks take flight,
I'm spinning like a dizzy kite!

The neighbors glance and shake their heads,
As I jive like I'm on beds.
With silly moves upon the floor,
I bring the laughter, never bore!

So here's to joy in swirling fright,
With plucky socks and dance delight.
In every mess, a chance to laugh,
I choose the fun – I'll take that path!

Lullabies of Tides Unfurled

The waves are crashing on the shore,
They serenade with water's roar.
I tiptoe in, a splashing fool,
While seagulls squawk, I play it cool.

With buckets full of sand and dreams,
I build a castle; it's bursting at the seams.
A crab crawls by, my new best friend,
In silly games, we twist and bend.

When tides come in, my fortress falls,
The crab just laughs, he knows it all.
Though soaked and soggy, I persevere,
For laughs and giggles bring good cheer!

With every splash and every wave,
I find the joy that turns me brave.
So let the tides both rise and churn,
For laughter's light is what I yearn!

Mirage of Gentle Warmth

The sun peeks in, a golden tease,
I'll bake like toast, if you please!
I lay down on the grass so green,
And dream of snacks, my belly's keen.

A funny sight, a duck in shade,
I watch it waddle, unafraid.
It quacks a tune, a silly song,
Together we sing, it can't be wrong!

The breeze is teasing, swoops and dives,
A frolic here, it makes me thrive.
With beer cans rolling down the lane,
I giggle hard; it drives me insane!

So let the warmth wrap 'round like hugs,
I'll chase the giggles, dodge the bugs.
In every ray that hits my skin,
I feel the fun is where I've been!

The Stillness Wrapped in Dusk

At dusk the fireflies bloom and peek,
I chase them down with giggles, meek.
Their tiny lights, a dance in air,
I trip and fall – oh, what a flare!

The moon rolls in, a silver disk,
While frogs begin their nightly brisk.
I join their chorus, croak and swell,
My off-key notes, a comedy well!

A snack in hand, I hear them croon,
In silly chats, the stars commune.
With marshmallows roasted to a fluff,
I've had my fill, but who's keeping up?

As shadows stretch and laughter grows,
The night unfolds in goofy shows.
In stillness wrapped, fun's here to stay,
With every grin, I find my way!

Traces of Calm in Morning Mist

The sun peeks out, a toddler's grin,
The world wakes up, let chaos begin!
Birds tweet gossip, squirrels chase their tails,
While coffee brews and sanity fails.

A fluffy cloud makes a fashion statement,
Winks at a tree, says, "Aren't we great?"
Pigeons strut like they own the street,
While I trip over my own two feet!

As dew drops sparkle like forgotten dreams,
Nature laughs, or so it seems.
With every giggle, a breeze so swift,
Morning's prank is nature's gift.

But here I stand, all lost and still,
Wondering if breakfast is worth the thrill.
Nature's smile, a secret feast,
In the misty calm, hilarity increased!

The Embrace of Time's Gentle Flow

Tick tock goes the wall clock's dance,
Time winks playfully, takes a chance.
Moments slip like butter on toast,
While I ponder what I miss the most.

A chair creaks louder than my thoughts,
Does it know my dreams are all for naught?
Time has a way of stealing socks,
Leaving only mismatched shocking flocks!

I chase the sun, but it has a laugh,
It moves faster than my morning half.
Yet in its glow, I find a grin,
A gentle reminder to breathe, begin.

So here's to moments that slip and slide,
Like a cat that refuses to abide.
In the flow of time, let's play a prank,
And fill our days with laughter's rank!

Fragments of Peace Amidst the Turmoil

A cat on a windowsill, strikes a pose,
Watching the world, as chaos grows.
Children run wild, a rollercoaster ride,
While I seek serenity, but it hides!

Traffic jams are like a dance gone wrong,
Horns blaring out their own silly song.
Yet in the chaos, a simple plea,
"Can I get a nap? Just let me be!"

In a tranquil park, I find my slice,
Squirrels barter acorns; they're quite precise.
With every nut and twinkle of cheer,
They giggle away my confusion and fear.

So let the world whirl in a merry spree,
I'll take my peace, with a sprinkle of glee.
In fragments of calm, a chuckle asked,
For harmony's smile, it wears a mask!

A Symphony of Grooves and Tranquility

The beat of life plays a jolly tune,
As I dance with dust bunnies, afternoon.
Each step a giggle, each twist a cheer,
Who knew my living room could hold such beer?

With pots and pans, I take the stage,
Conducting chaos like a wise old sage.
Neighbors peek out, a curious crowd,
Am I dancing alone? Or am I proud?

Every misstep has its own sweet flair,
As laughter echoes through the air.
With melodies that tickle our spine,
Even a wrong note feels utterly divine!

So join this symphony, wild and free,
In grooves of joy, there's always me.
With every laugh, the world spins bright,
A concert of whimsy, from day to night!

Meditation under Moonlight

In the glow of night, I sit and wait,
My thoughts all waltzing, oh isn't fate?
The moon is laughing, a giant smile,
I'm hoping for wisdom, though it's been a while.

Crickets croon a melody quite absurd,
While I ponder life, they don't say a word.
Breezes tease my hair, like a playful friend,
This tranquil moment seems to never end.

But as I'm lost in thoughts so deep,
I hear a rustle, oh what a leap!
A raccoon stops by, with a snack in hand,
Meditation's shifted, now it's 'who can stand?'

Lunar shines down, my giggles arise,
As critters join me, under the skies.
I swear this is deep thought, I can't deny,
While munching my chips, oh me, oh my!

Ebb and Flow of Silence

In quiet moments, my thoughts drift away,
Like waves of the ocean, they frolic and play.
A to-do list forms, but it soon takes flight,
As my cat purrs loudly—oh what a delight!

The stillness surrounds me, but not for long,
A squirrel outside sings an off-key song.
I try to focus, give stillness a chance,
But my thoughts are now doing a silly dance.

A laugh in the air, I can't help but snort,
As a flock of birds rolls in for support.
They decide to chirp, and add to the fun,
Reminding me silence, well, has come undone.

So here I sit, in this riot of peace,
Nature's own sitcom, a cheeky release.
I raise my hands up, give it all a cheer,
In this hilarious hush, I know I belong here!

Nature's Breath in Stillness

In the heart of the woods, a silence is found,
With trees all around, and a soft, bouncy ground.
I breathe in the air, it smells like pine cones,
But then a squirrel throws a nut, and I groan!

Each rustle and whimper, though meant to be peace,
Creates a cacophony that will not cease.
A butterfly lands on my nose with a chuckle,
While nearby a deer tries to hide in a shuffle.

'What's this place?' I think, as I try to unwind,
A nature retreat, of the funniest kind.
Leaves joke around, whispering sweet nothings,
While I trip over roots as they hold back their chucklings.

But laughter surrounded, this stillness is rare,
With every small creature embracing the air.
I crack up with joy at the sights so bizarre,
Nature's the comedian, the world is the star!

A Symphony of Soft Shadows

Under soft shadows, I lay in repose,
But quickly, I sense an itch on my nose.
A tickling breeze turns into a sneeze,
And suddenly shadows are giggling with ease.

The twilight brings whispers, a chatter so bright,
As fireflies dance like they've partied all night.
I try to relax, yet the world seems to shout,
With owls who hoot jokes that they can't live without.

My blanket is cozy, but it plays tricks too,
It wraps me up tight; oh, how will I move?
But shadows just laugh as I wiggle and twist,
As crickets all snicker—'Oh dear, such a tryst!'

With laughter in layers, the darkness unveils,
A symphony played in the wind's breezy tales.
So here in the night, with the shadows around,
I find joy in the chaos, where laughter is found.

Reflections in the Still Waters

In pools where ducks wear hats so grand,
A splashy dance on water land.
They quack with glee, a jolly sight,
While fish swim by, dodging their delight.

Bobbing boats with tiny sails,
Chasing dreams on aquatic trails.
The frogs strike poses, like movie stars,
In a show where laughter's never far.

Uncle Joe tries to skip a stone,
But lands it straight in his own bone.
With a laugh we gather 'round,
In this comedic watery sound.

So here we sit, as night unfurls,
With little jokes and giggly swirls.
The moon reflects on chuckles bright,
As stars peek in, what a funny night!

The Poetry of Endless Horizons.

Kites soar high like birds in flight,
While I stand still, grasping tight.
With tangled strings and flailing shrieks,
I join the dance, all clumsy peaks.

In fields where daisies wear big bows,
The sun teases, it surely knows.
I trip on roots, a classic move,
While giggling bugs start to groove.

The clouds above make shapes and jokes,
A fluffy cow, a herd of folks.
With every sigh and playful swoosh,
We laugh till breath is hard to push.

And as the shadows stretch and bend,
We share our tales, a noisy blend.
In this grand space where silliness roams,
The horizon's vast, yet we're all home!

Whispers of the Desert Breeze

The breeze calls out with silly rhymes,
Tickling toes through endless climes.
A tumbleweed begins to dance,
While lizards laugh, giving a glance.

Cacti wear hats, a festive scene,
As coyotes howl, what a routine!
Prickly pear sings a pointy song,
While tumbleweeds roll, bustling along.

The sun slips lower in the sky,
While mischief stirs, oh me, oh my!
Sand in my pants, what a plight,
Still giggles rise with all our might.

The mystical winds invite us near,
With every gust, more giggles here.
As evening lights begin to fade,
We pack our laughs, the perfect trade.

Tranquil Dunes in Twilight

The dunes wave gently, a beachside caress,
Where seagulls squawk and create a mess.
Footprints dance on the golden grains,
While children giggle, ignoring the pains.

A sandcastle stands, a royal decree,
With jellybean guards who won't let me flee.
The tides roll in and splash our toes,
As the tide tries to tickle, we giggle and pose.

Sunset spills colors, a laughter parade,
With marshmallow clouds that never invade.
Shells whisper secrets, stories in glee,
As we share tales with a giggling spree.

So here's to the dusk, so lively and bright,
With grains of joy, we take flight.
In twilight's embrace, we find our cheer,
As the waves sing softly, we'll always be here.

The Last Glow of the Day's Farewell

The sun dips low, what a sight,
Its rays take turns—oh, what a fight!
A squirrel dons sunglasses, quite the flair,
While crickets giggle without a care.

The clouds wear pink, like cotton candy,
As birds hold court, so sweet and dandy.
With every second, the light does waltz,
Even the sunset cannot help but pulse.

Gentle Embrace of Dusk's Shadows

The shadows stretch and play a game,
A tussle of shapes with no one to blame.
A cat attempts to catch the night,
But naps instead—what a silly sight!

As fireflies flicker, my worries wane,
Dusk giggles softly, 'Never complain!'
With every glance, the dark feels bright,
As chaos swirls, it's pure delight.

Essence of Tranquility in Every Grain

Tiny grains twinkle like stars on the floor,
A beach ball rolls and starts a roar.
A crab in shorts dances in glee,
While waves get jealous, quite a sight to see!

Seagulls squawk with a comedic flair,
Thinking they're cool, without a care.
As laughter drifts with the salty breeze,
Each grain chuckles, happy as can be.

A Tapestry of Silence under Starlight

Stars gossip quietly, oh what a scene,
While moonbeams weave a magical sheen.
Bats in tuxedos flit and glide,
Making the night a joyful ride!

A rabbit wears spectacles, all suave and neat,
Reading a book, oh what a feat!
With every twinkle, the night plays along,
In this whimsical world, we all belong.

Secrets Unfolding Beneath Sunny Skies

In the garden, gnomes take shifts,
With hats so bright, they trade their gifts.
A squirrel plans a heist all day,
While bees hold raves in a polline sway.

The lawn chairs gossip under their shade,
About the time the cat mislaid.
A rubber duck floats, like a king,
Imagining crowns and pigeon wings.

A pie on the sill just begged to dive,
While ants argue over how to thrive.
The sun just giggles, setting the tone,
For all the silly tales to be known.

And when the dusk folds its arms tight,
The garden laughs 'til the stars ignite.
For secrets dwell where the humor grows,
In the land where everyone knows!

Ephemeral Shadows in Sunlit Valleys

In valleys where the shadows waltz,
A cow in sunglasses, oh what a pulse!
Chasing butterflies with a daring grin,
While goats argue over who wears the win.

The rabbits hold a race on the track,
With carrots as prizes—get ready, Jack!
Each hop a giggle, each leap a jest,
The race of the critters is surely the best.

A wind-chime sings songs that tickle the ear,
As crickets narrate tales we all want to hear.
The shadows play tag, running 'round trees,
While frogs conduct symphonies with ease.

As twilight falls with a wink and nod,
The valleys chuckle, 'tis a quirky facade!
For in each giggle, the shadows are grand,
In a world so silly, come take my hand!

The Language of the Quiet Breeze

A whispering rush, the breeze doth speak,
Sharing secrets that tickle the cheek.
It teases the leaves, a playful tease,
While flowers giggle, swaying with ease.

A butterfly flutters, a wink on its flight,
As the breeze tells the sun, "You're looking quite bright!"

The clouds above chuckle, puffy and round,
While daisies make jokes that never confound.

Alas, the zephyr sends twigs on their quest,
To see which can balance on flowers the best.
The dance of the breeze, oh what a delight,
As laughter and whispers wrap up the night.

With every gust, there's a giggling sigh,
A language of joy that floats in the sky.
Embrace the soft tickles, the chuckles to seize,
In the realm of whispers, the heart finds its ease.

A Pilgrimage to Quiet Shores

To shores where flip-flops forever flop,
Where seagulls cackle and never stop.
In the sandcastles, a monarch reigns,
While crabs march like soldiers in lines that are twains.

The sun is a jester, playing its part,
As kids splash waves, soaking each heart.
The shells on the beach gossip and chatter,
While a fish in a bucket thinks life really matters.

A turtle in shades makes a real slow run,
Clearing a path for the setting sun.
As kites in the air perform acrobatics,
The ocean laughs—what a bunch of theatrics!

As the dusk unfolds its soft, warm embrace,
With footprints in sand, a giggly trace.
We find that to wander brings peace, yes indeed,
In the shores full of joy where laughter is freed!

Ebb and Flow of Timeless Dreams

Waves of giggles roll like tides,
As dreams chase night with silly slides.
In the moon's glow, tales we weave,
With laughter echoing, we believe.

A crab in a top hat makes a scene,
With polka-dot shorts, he's quite the queen.
Jellyfish dancing with a gleeful swish,
Even the starfish wishes for a dish.

Whims of the Wind Through Whispering Grains

The breezy giggle of the grass,
Tickles the toes when you dash past.
Kites dive low, playing hooky,
While bushes giggle, all quite kooky.

A tumbleweed does the cha-cha slide,
As the sun dips low, it takes a ride.
Chasing clouds in a feathered hat,
While squirrels join in, fancy that!

Luminescent Dreams on Soft Land

Glowworms shine like tiny stars,
Frogs in jammies try to be czars.
With each leap, they take a bow,
The moon giggles, oh, look at them now!

Bubbles float like wishes in the blue,
As fireflies change into a crew.
With popcorn trees, we munch and crunch,
Awaiting the next dreamy lunch!

Quiet Footfalls on Endless Paths

In the hush, the path hums a tune,
As turtles race by, donned in a moon.
With every step, a laugh escapes,
While ants discuss the latest capes.

Beneath the stars, we frolic and play,
Socks on our heads, we dance in ballet.
Whispers of joy in every stride,
On ticklish trails, we'll forever glide.

Night's Breath on the Desert's Skin

Under the stars, a cactus sighed,
A tumbleweed's dance, the night just cried.
Beneath a moon, the lizards prance,
As owls hoot softly, in a game of chance.

The dunes wear shadows, a playful disguise,
While mischievous snakes twist with surprise.
A lone jackrabbit hops, so spry and spruced,
While scorpions chuckle, feeling quite juiced.

Stars tumble down, in the warm night air,
Dust devils compete in a wild, silly dare.
Sand in my shoes, a constant plight,
But the desert's giggles make it feel right.

Underneath laughter, the night unfolds,
With stories of camels and gold-plated molds.
The warm wind whistles a quirky tune,
As night whispers secrets to the lazy moon.

Serenity in the Heart of Motion

A cactus on wheels, what a sight to see,
Rolling along, quite carefree and free.
The wind in its spines, a joyful breeze,
Who needs a chair when you've got such ease?

Tumbleweeds twirl, in a soft ballet,
They laugh and they tumble, come what may.
In this moving madness, where chaos reigns,
Even the lizards are bursting with gains.

Traveling through mirage, with winks and grins,
The sun turns up, bringing shimmering sins.
Every moment's a giggle, a warm sunny flirt,
While the friends on the road all wear sand for a shirt.

So let's dance in the dust, with plenty of zest,
Life is a riot, a fun-loving quest.
Our hearts filled with giggles, our shoes feeling light,
In a whirlwind of motion, we take our flight!

The Rhythm of Quiet Footsteps

Whispers of sand under feet so bold,
Each step a giggle, a story untold.
The dunes' soft giggles, in breeze they play,
A playful procession, leading our way.

Cacti are cheering, a fine audience,
As I dance past them, they join the romance.
A tumbleweed rolls, tries to keep in step,
With rhythm so wild, there's no need for prep.

Footprints record all the laughter I weave,
Each shuffle a memory, what joy to believe!
I hop over shadows, full of delight,
The desert's my stage, in the warm, sweet night.

With every footprint, a jester's delight,
I twirl in the sand, all through the night.
Nature jests back, oh, what a show,
The quietest dance, still makes the heart glow!

Sunkissed Reflections on Travelled Paths

Golden light shimmers on paths I've roamed,
As mirage plays tricks on the eye, so homed.
A squirrel flips out, stealing my snack,
While I try to eat, and not lose my track.

Beneath the sun's smile, I leap with a grin,
Sandals are happy, oh, the joy from within!
My shadow's a dancer, all twisty and fun,
Laughing behind me, 'til the day is done.

Every glance at the horizon's embrace,
Tickles my senses, makes me lose pace.
Tracks that I've followed, like trails of a joke,
Every footfall a laugh, as the day bids adieu.

Travelled paths lead me to moments so sweet,
With laughter around me and sand beneath feet.
Catch a glimpse of the funny, in places unseen,
In the warm sunlight, life's a comical scene!

Elysian Echoes at Day's End

When the sun yawns low and drowsy,
The seagulls squawk like they're too noisy.
Flip-flops flip with erratic grace,
As children chase waves, a comical race.

In the distance, a sandcastle crumbles,
A proud architect, he simply grumbles.
Jellyfish float like jelly on toast,
While beachgoers sunbathe, their dreams are lost.

Umbrella shades twirl, like they're on a spree,
Dancing with wind, oh what a sight to see!
Laughter bubbles up, a frothy delight,
Kites tumble and loop, chasing the light.

With each sunset yearning, we cheer and applaud,
To the fleeting moments, we take a nod.
In this echo of joy where life finds a way,
We embrace each mistake, 'cause it's all in the play.

The Alchemy of Calm and Chaos

In the mix of buttery popcorn and sun,
Chaos erupts when the ice cream's done.
Sandy toes tap to a rhythm absurd,
As seagulls squabble, not caring a word.

A beach chair flips with a humor-filled gust,
Leaving behind dignity, laughter is a must.
Waves crash like giggles on shores oh-so-brave,
While sunbathers flop in a colorful wave.

The frisbee's trajectory, defying all laws,
Bounces off my forehead! Applause, applause!
With toe-sunburned noses, we cackle aloud,
This blend of sunshine, chaos, we're proud.

As day fades away like a quirky old clown,
We wink at the sunset, no need for a frown.
In the alchemy of giggles and sun's golden rays,
We mix memories lively, in joyful arrays.

Gentle Harbors of the Mind

In a hammock, I sway, an enchanting delight,
While ants throw a party, what a silly sight!
Coconuts gossip, swung low on the trees,
Tickling the breeze, busting out laughing with ease.

Crabs dance sideways, with no sense of time,
In a comical world where rhythm's a mime.
Flip-flops are lost, in a sandy embrace,
Who knew that footwear could vanish with grace?

A cooler pops open, it sounds like a song,
Beverages tumble, it won't be long.
In a feast of joy, the laughter will blend,
With salty sea snacks, on that we depend.

We welcome the evening with goofy grins found,
As the stars pop out, shooting joy all around.
In this gentle harbor, where giggles unwind,
We sail off to dreams, leaving worries behind.

Interludes of Peace in the Chaos

Between the giggles and splashes galore,
Peace sneaks in, and we're ready for more.
A beach ball bounces, but misses its mark,
Rolling away, it's off to the park.

Sunscreen battles with sand, a messy affair,
Like children, we wrestle without a care.
Towels tangle like octopuses' arms,
In this delightful chaos, we find all the charms.

Ice cream drips down with a splat and a grin,
A sticky situation that's destined to win.
Splash zones erupt with laughter galore,
As waves chase us back, in the sun's playful roar.

When the sky dims, and stars start to peek,
We gather our treasures and feel quite unique.
In these interludes loaded with joy and some strife,
We swirl in the madness, that's the spice of life!

Cerulean Skies Unraveled

A bird with glasses flies by,
Singing tunes that make us sigh.
Pigeon gossip fills the air,
With tales of who snatched the pear.

A sunbeam tickles a snoozing cat,
She dreams of fish and an old top hat.
Clouds are fluffier than grandma's cake,
Floating by with dreamy wake.

The daisies dance, a comedy show,
In the breeze, they put on a glow.
Laughter spills from a nearby stream,
Wishing to join in the whimsical dream.

As the sky blushes a silly hue,
We giggle at what the day will brew.
With each gleeful twist and turn,
Life is a laugh, and oh, how we learn!

A Tapestry of Still Waters

A frog in a vest takes a leap,
Into the pond where secrets creep.
He plops and splashes, oh what a cheer,
The fish all laugh, it's time for beer!

Lilies gossip, dressed in white,
Whispering tales until late at night.
The moon winks at a shy great egrett,
Pretending he's cooler than we all get.

The mirror water holds a prank,
Reflecting faces, none but a prank.
A duck quacks loud, "I'm the king!"
While lily pads dance, doing their fling.

Ripples ripple, laughter spreads,
As turtles use logs for their beds.
Nature's stage is a wild affair,
A circus with creatures beyond compare!

Beneath a Starlit Veil

Fireflies play hide and seek,
Dancing around my old teddy peak.
Stars twinkle like a bunch of lights,
Winking at us from far-off heights.

A raccoon debonair in a tie,
Sniffs out secrets as he strolls by.
"Is there pizza in your picnic basket?"
He asks while wearing a foolish mask-it!

Crickets chirp the evening's tune,
While owls talk of the great monsoon.
A coyote howls a goofy song,
Making the night feel wild and strong.

Time to lay beneath this show,
Where silliness steals the afterglow.
With the moonlight as our only guide,
We laugh till dawn, hearts open wide!

The Breath of the Earth

The grass tickles, giggles abound,
As ants parade in their small town.
Each blade a tickler, like nature's tease,
Prompting us to giggle with ease.

Upon the hill, a sheep named Lou,
Tries on glasses, says, "I see you!"
He memes with clouds, oh how they laugh,
As they share their fluffy photograph!

A garden gnome with a silly beard,
Tripped on a flower, but never feared.
He told the daisies, "Don't you fret,
I'm just warming up for the sunset!"

Each breeze a chuckle, every leaf a cheer,
Nature's humor is always near.
With every step, the joy does swell,
In this lively bubble, we dwell!

Threads of Time in Serenity's Veil

Tick-tock goes the clock, but I stay late,
Laughter dances like waves on a plate.
A cat in a hat thinks he's a sage,
But it's just a costume, a clever gauge.

Tickles of time in a hammock rest,
Sipping lemonade like I'm royally blessed.
Why does that seagull snatch my fries?
As if he knows life's all about the prize!

Jumpy dreams weave with laughter bright,
Who knew that tatering could feel so right?
Like juggling pineapples in a parade,
Every silly moment in sun's golden shade.

The Gentle Pull of Perspective's Anchor

Hangovers from cheese puffs and fries,
But my favorite view still makes me rise.
An anchor of laughter, a buoy of cheer,
Skateboarding with pigeons, let's flip in gear!

Nice flip-flops adorned with polka dots,
Dancing with shadows, we care not what's hot.
The world's a circus, the show's our ticket,
In this jester's life, we'll laugh 'til we're sicket!

A fish in a bowtie gives me a wink,
In this world of weirdness, we hardly think.
I might just wear socks with my sandals too,
Life's anchor holds, through funny and true.

Where Dreams Drift on Whispered Winds

Kites tied to dreams, soaring high and bold,
While I chase my thoughts, all shiny and gold.
A cloud with a grin, it tickles my nose,
Teasing me gently as the wild wind blows.

Hot air balloons with faces of glee,
I jump on this ride, oh what fun to see!
Sipping on bubbles filled with pink cheer,
A dream in the sky, let's all disappear!

A quirky parade of thoughts on a string,
Waddling with nonsense, oh what joy they bring!
Like snappy alligators in polka-dot hats,
Drifting where laughter and silliness chats.

Sunlit Echoes on Tranquil Waters

Reflections of giggles ripple with grace,
Like ducks in a row sporting a smiley face.
Sunlit whispers bounce off the lake,
As I slip on a fish-suit for laughter's sake!

The rays tease the water, it shimmers and plays,
Splashing my thoughts in the sun's vibrant rays.
A turtle's slow pace, he chuckles with me,
Racing on waves as they sparkle with glee!

Oh, how the ripples do giggle and dance,
The fish tell their tales, give me a chance!
In the echo of sunlight, joy's written clear,
Who knew calm moments could tickle the ear?

The Song of the Gentle Breeze

A breeze so light, it tickles my nose,
Whispering secrets, as it playfully flows.
It dances with leaves, a giggling delight,
Turning my frown into pure laughter's flight.

Clouds line up like a funny parade,
Wobbling and swaying, they can't seem to fade.
I chase them with glee, in this game of wits,
While the sun beams a grin, as my happiness sits.

Oh, how the flowers join in the sprightly fun,
Dressed in bright colors, they shine like the sun.
They wink as I pass, in their comical ways,
Nature's jesters, bringing joy to my days.

A wave of laughter, it rolls like the sea,
In the humorous heart of this merry spree.
With each gentle gust, my worries depart,
This playful breeze tickles my grateful heart.

Moments Carved in Time

Tick-tock goes the clock, with a chuckle and grin,
Like a comedian's act, it's a whimsical spin.
Every second it laughs, draws a giggle or two,
While memories bloom, like a pop of bright hue.

Snapshots of joy, like selfies gone wrong,
Captured in frames where we all belt out songs.
A mishap on video, we're clumsy and bold,
Still, our hearts stay warm, like a treasure of gold.

Each moment a sketch, of a life full of cheer,
In the art of the silly, we find joy so dear.
Though colors may blend, in a humorous strife,
We laugh at the canvas, the portrait of life.

So here's to the moments, both silly and bright,
Each tick brings the joy, that makes everything right.
We'll dance through the days, with a wink and a nudge,
In this quirky adventure, we all hold a grudge.

Tides of Tranquility

The waves shimmy in jest, like a playful dog,
Barking at the shore, in a silly bog.
They leap with glee, in a splashy embrace,
While I steal a glance at their frothy face.

Seagulls applaud with a mock-loud cheer,
As they pirouette gracefully, without any fear.
They dive for their snacks, like clowns in a show,
With antics galore, putting on quite the flow.

The sun dips low, a clown in its prime,
Painting the sky in a carnival rhyme.
Each hue a giggle, as day meets the night,
With laughter echoing, a pocket of light.

So come, take a dip in this playful array,
Where humor and tides dance in bright dismay.
For even the ocean knows how to joke,
In this vast playground where laughter's no hoax.

The Architecture of Calm

In a world of stillness, the breezes collide,
Building laughter's arches, no need to hide.
The structures of joy rise high in the sky,
With bricks made of giggles, they'll never say bye.

Pillars of patience, they sway and they bend,
Standing tall like jesters, they never pretend.
Crafting towers of chuckles, with walls made of cheer,
Each window a wink, inviting us near.

Roofs made of sunshine, the most comical beams,
With shadows that play, igniting our dreams.
Staircases of humor lead up to the clouds,
Where laughter echoes freely, breaking all shrouds.

So visit this structure of silvery light,
Where calm meets the funny, and everything's bright.
In this quirky domain, we learn to let go,
Building bridges with humor, creating life's flow.

Reflections in the Golden Hour

The sun dips low, a clumsy show,
It trips on clouds, and then it bows.
A seagull's squawk, a startled crow,
Take your picture—oh! Not so slow!

The waves are giggling at my feet,
They tickle toes like a sneaky greet.
With every splash, I can't compete,
As sand sticks tight, it's quite the feat!

A crab, he dances in a line,
Proclaims his kingdom, feels divine.
But wait! He slips on sticky brine,
And chuckles softly—it's so fine!

With golden hues, the day will fade,
But laughter lingers in the shade.
We'll share our jokes, and they won't lade,
As twilight winks, and fun is made!

Solace Beneath the Half-Moon

A lunar smile lights up the night,
I trip on shadows, what a sight!
The ocean sings, the tides invite,
But watch your step! It's quite the fright!

The stars above, they wink and tease,
As crabs all dance with utmost ease.
In twilight's glow, they prance like peas,
I join their cup—oh, pass the cheese!

The half-moon giggles, quite the jest,
It flicks its beams—it loves the best.
But here comes trouble, dressed in quest,
I spill my drink—oh, such unrest!

Yet laughter fills this sandy shore,
With every bump, I crave for more.
And moonlight whispers like before,
Our funny tales, they sweetly soar!

The Dance of Grain and Light

The grains of light do shimmy and sway,
While I attempt to dance and play.
But every step seems lost, I say,
As sand embraces—come what may!

I twirl and swirl with wild delight,
While beach towels whack in the bright twilight.
A seagull joins, it takes to flight,
A dance-off now? What a fine sight!

The waves, they pulse in joyous pride,
As I fall down, I can't abide.
The laughter echoes, none can hide,
In every tumble, smiles collide!

A grainy mess? Oh, yes indeed,
But laughter's the finest kind of seed.
We sprout new jokes with perfect speed,
As fun ignites, it's all we need!

Serene Horizons at Dusk

The sunset splashes colors wide,
While I'm caught in a flip-flop slide.
I laugh out loud—oh, what a ride,
As gentle waves become my guide!

The horizon's blush, a rosy face,
While crabs scuttle, they set the pace.
With every splash, I find my place,
In smiles that light the sandy space!

The twilight's glow makes shadows dance,
I misstep thrice, it's pure romance.
But in this blunder, life's second chance,
As laughter flares—a silly stance!

So here I sit, with friends galore,
With funny tales from every shore.
As dusk wraps 'round, we crave much more,
With joy that lingers—let's explore!

www.ingramcontent.com/pod-product-compliance
Lightning Source LLC
Chambersburg PA
CBHW072135070526
44585CB00016B/1691